# How To Avoid Getting Raped

Christopher Robinson

ISBN:10:1463618964
ISBN-13:978-1463618964

# DEDICATION

This book is dedicated to all the women who has being victims of rape and to their families who have been traumatized by the act, yet continued to give support.

To all my female mentors: my daughter Shauna, sisters Tracy-Ann, Letisha and Ann-Marie. My mother Christabelle-Elaine, grand-mother Lenna and Mrs. Clover Wilson my editor, to all my nieces, my friend Shereen Anecia Myrie who I keep awake many nights, Kimone Sedoney Malcolm who tolerate me and her beautiful daughter Deborah Lisa Marie special love and thanks, Sandra Hines who keep me sane, Marcella Reid who make me laugh like crazy each time I see her.

# CONTENTS

# INTRODUCTION

The Good Book says " An ounce of prevention is better than a pound of cure." To be forewarned is to be forearmed. This book contains positive information to help combat the crime of rape and the terrorism brought on by would be rapists.

Statistics show that there has been a sixty-seven percent increase in the number of reported cases of rape worldwide from January to October 2008 compared to the period in 2007.

God forbid that someone should try to rape you, but if there is an attempt, you would be prepared. Reading this book would be of tremendous help, so avoid hurt, pain and psychological trauma. Arm yourself with a copy of this book.

DEVON HALL

# ACKNOWLEDGMENTS

My heartfelt thanks to my friends and Master Mind group. Without them this book would not be possible: David Walters, Royston Loutin, Errol Usher, Devon Hall, Kenneth Straw, Ervin Bennett, Paul Bennett, Marlon Morrison, Radcliff Narine, Andrew Gillspie, Andrew Wilson, Norman Wallace, Peter Simmonds and Biggs.

To my father Donald Lee Robinson-thanks for believing in me, my brother thanks for your continued love and support.

To my son Ghaijhuian—you are my joy my life.

# CHAPTER ONE

## DEFENSES AGAINST RAPE

Rape is not a sex crime, but a crime of violence that includes dominating and imposing power or will over the victim. Victims of this crime are primarily women. It is a crime greatly misunderstood by most people, men and women alike.

More than any other crime, the physical and psychological effects of rape tend to be long lasting. Rape carries with it the immediate physical dangers of being beaten, injured or killed, as well as the possibility of pregnancy or sexually transmitted diseases including AIDS.

The victim is also subjected to psychological stress and trauma that may last for a lifetime. The rape victims often feel humiliated and ostracized. These consequences are compounded by prevailing community attitudes towards the victims of rape.

Rape is a crime that affects everyone. No man, woman or child is exempt from being a victim. EIGHTY PERCENT OF VICTIMS KNOW THEIR ATTACKER (THE RAPIST).

Attitudes towards rape vary greatly. Men have a considerably different view of rape from women. Typical comments, easily identifiable by gender, range from "A woman can run faster with her skirt up than a man with his pants down" to "castration should be a mandatory penalty for any rape conviction.

Rape is defined as "to carnally know and forcibly ravish a person against his or her will.

## IF YOU ARE ATTACKED

Since self protective measures help in the majority of attack, to whatever extent you are temperamentally and emotionally capable, you should be prepared to defend yourself physically.

If you are not serious about, or simply not capable of inflicting pain or physical harm on your assailant, you should not attempt it. If you are determined to defend yourself, you should remember that your best defense is ESCAPE. Remember that legs are made to run, and voices are to scream. High heeled shoes can be used to kick at an assailant. His natural reaction will be to duck, being unbalance may give the victim the chance to run.

The best time to make a break for escape is early during the assault as possible, the moment to react is during the first twenty seconds. The attacker won't expect an escape then. Also the less time you are under the control of the rapist, the less likely you are to be hurt or intimidated. Moreover, your chances of escape are better before the rapist gains total control and before he has the chance to throw you to the ground, or force you to a secluded spot.

The longer you submit passively to the attacker's demands, the less likely you are to react later on. Fear of antagonizing your assailant will worsen, and overcoming inertia will become more difficult over time.

Scream and run and in case your voice fails you, keep a whistle strapped on to your wrist. It will make noise when your voice might not. Some people have suggested that screaming "fire" rather than "help!" might bring assistance more quickly. Yelling will also distract the rapist and alert others of the danger. A powerful, energized, firm, loud scream sends a signal to the assailant that he likely had picked the wrong target.

Hysterics are not recommended, because this may cause the assailant to panic and communicate to him your fear and vulnerability.

If you are trapped and have little chance of escape, should you fight or not? A woman will tell you to fight; a man will tell you not to. If you do fight, statistics indicate that you will be attacked physically, have your arm twisted or suffer a brutal beating. The best policy is never to fight an assailant armed with a gun or a knife. But if his only weapon is superior strength, your chance of avoiding being raped by resisting is probably worth taking. Only you can decide whether and how to resist a rape attack, and since every situation is different, no one can second guess you.

Female victims of violent assault who defended themselves are less likely to be injured than those who plead with the attacker or who offered no resistance.

In general, a rape victim must resist her attacker. Lacking this, there may be charges of consenting sexual intercourse. However, the resistance need not be physical to say, " I don't want to do that. Please don't make me do that," clearly establishes resistance. There is however the distinct possibility that your attacker will contradict this in court.

If, on the other hand, you physically attacked your assailant, leaving cuts and contusions on him, you have gone far in establishing your retaliation in kind.

You may be able to change the rapist's intentions. He may be reluctant to have sexual contact with you if he believes you have a sexually transmitted disease. You may be able to persuade the rapist that you want to have a sexual relationship with him, but in a more comfortable setting.

Pretend to invite him to your place, with the intention of escaping or summoning assistance. Try to make yourself unattractive by telling him you are at the peak of your menstrual period or you have stomach cramps. This may distract the assailant or perhaps cause him to loosen his grip. Some women have vomited or relieved themselves to ward off a persistent assailant, and others have been successful feigning mental retardation.

# CHAPTER TWO

## DEFENSIVE WEAPONS AND TATICS

"If you have a weapon, you may even swing the odds in your favor." Weapons include but are not limited to small knives, mace, hat pins, a pencil, a corkscrew, pepper, lemon juice in a squeeze bottle, or even a ring clenched in the fist with keys protruding between the fingers. All of these can be used against the attacker's eyes. An umbrella can be a good weapon if used like a spear or sword rather than a club.

However, you should be warned; many men have had some boxing or other self-defense training, and your assailant may be able to block your swings. Even so, his reversal from offensive to defensive tactics may give you a chance to flee, and if you are lucky, you'll at least discourage him from his initial objective. But remember, if you do attack, be prepared to keep it up.

Some authorities will tell you to attack your assailant in the groin area. While this is his most vulnerable spot, he is also likely to protect this area, both through instinct and from a lifetime of training. Instead go for the pit of the stomach, the throat, the eyes, the temples or even the kneecap. Other vulnerable and easily accessible parts of the body include the kidneys, solar plexus, little finger, nose and ears. However, if the rapist should make an embracing type of attack to the front, then a knee to the groin might be effective, or grab his scrotum in the groin area with hands, squeeze, twist, and drop to the ground so the full weight of your body is on his scrotum. This technique should disable the attacker.

Some experts recommend a well placed, close-fisted thrust aimed at the trachea or Adam's apple, while at the same time using your other hand to pull the rapist's, while at the same time using your other hand to pull the rapist's head forward. Correct implementation of this technique is highly likely to disable the assailant, or cup your hands and with all your might, in one continuous sweeping motion, strike your assailant's ears and then forcefully press both thumbs into his eyes. This tactic is particularly useful when the rapist is facing you and pressing you toward him.

If you are grabbed from the rear, an elbow to the stomach can be effective in getting you free. Stomping on the attackers foot, especially with high-heeled shoes, can easily break his foot. Try to hit about halfway between the ankle and the shoes. The pain of this might well discourage any further attack. Even if it doesn't it might make it easier for you to break free and run.

Other aggressive actions include eye gouging, biting, scratching and kicking. Additional natural weapons include your head, heel, the palm of your hands, thumbs, hips and the forearms. The rapist will usually try to throw you to the ground, your chances of defense are lessened but not hopeless. For the best chance of defending yourself, take a self-defense course that is geared to help women defend themselves from such threatening situations. If however you are trapped and so threatened that you cannot escape, you may still be able to avoid attack by doing nothing more than crying, which should not be too difficult under the circumstances. There could be circumstances, moreover, which may make it impossible for you to resist. If for example he threatens not you, but your child, you may feel there is no alternative but to accede to his demands. No matter what we, or anyone may advise you, the decisions you make when face to face with an attacker must be yours, and must be based on circumstances as you see them. Your body will release chemicals into your bloodstream that will help you fight, or outsmart your attacker. Once the incident is over, and you meditate on what you did and how you might have done otherwise, remember that your actions dictated by your body as well as your mind and if you had to do it all over again, it would probably have turned out the same way. For the best chance of defending yourself, take a self-defense course that is geared to help women defend themselves from such threatening situations. If however you are trapped and so threatened that you cannot escape, you may still be able to avoid attack by doing nothing more that crying, which should not be too difficult under the circumstances. There could be circumstances, moreover, which may make it impossible for you to resist. If for example he threatens not you, but your child you may feel there is no alternative but to accede to his demands. No matter what we or anyone may advise you, the decisions you make when face to face with an attacker must be yours, and must be based on circumstances as you see them. Your body will release chemicals into your bloodstream that will help you fight, run, or outsmart your attacker.

Once the incident is over, and you meditate on what you did and how you might have done otherwise, remember that your actions were dictated by your body as well as your mind, and if you had to do it all over again, it would probably have turned out the same way.

AFTERMATH: Feelings of Rape Victims:

Unlike the victims of most other crimes, the victims of rape will experience lingering emotional effects.

FEAR: During a rape, victims believe that, in addition to the sexual assault, they are going to be brutally beaten or even murdered. Often the rapist threatens to assault again if the victim goes to the police or threatens to expose the assailants' identity.

GUILT: many women feel guilty after being raped, because they somehow believe that they are to be blamed for having been raped. This feeling of guilt often prevents a rape victim from reporting the crime to the police.

LOSS OF CONTROL: rape victims often feel loss of control over their own lives, because they were forced to submit to an act they consider abhorrent. They may reason that 'just as the rapist overcame my resistance by force, anyone can persuade me to do anything.' It becomes difficult for the victim to make decisions about simple matters.

EMBARASSMENT: rape victims are often embarrassed to discuss the physical and psychological details of the assault.

ANGER: A healthier and more appropriate response is anger. The victim has been attacked, demeaned and humiliated. She may express anger by telling other women about the attack or by pressing charge. She may also generalize and extend her anger and mistrust to all men.

A SENSE OF INFERIORITY: Victims may wonder why the rapist chose them. These feelings are related to the widespread, but false belief, which those who are raped "asked for it."


THE DECISION TO REPORT A RAPE

Once a rape is over, only you can decide to report it. But failure to prosecute encourages the rapist to try again.

## DEFENSES AGAINST RAPE

1. A female must resist a rapist, but not necessarily physically. "Don't make me do it" is a plea that indicates duress.
2. Write down or tape-record all incidents while they are still fresh in your mind.
3. Do not bathe, change clothes, douche, or otherwise clean up after an attack. You may be destroying evidence. Take a change of clothing with you when you go to file the report, because the clothing you were wearing might be required for evidence.
4. Carry everyday items for use as defensive weapons: pens or pencils, red pepper, lemon juice in a squeeze bottle, a key ring or an umbrella.
5. Attack an assailant at the throat, stomach, temples, eyes, kneecaps, or other vulnerable points.
6. Use a knee to the groin if an assailant makes an embarrassing attack from the front.
7. Stomp on the assailant's foot, at the instep, as a defensive measure.
8. Deliver a sharp blow to the stomach  with an elbow if you are attacked from the rear.
9. Be aware that a date could degenerate into a rape, maintain defenses at all times.

10. Try an emotional appeal if escape or resistance is impossible or impractical. By crying or attempting conversation, you may thwart an attack or lessen its severity.

11. Undergo the required physician's examination and consider having another from your gynecologist.

12. The decision to resist or not, is soley up to the victim. The decision must be based on circumstances existing at the time of the attack.

13. Seek counseling or other professional help as soon as you are able.

14. Above all, remember that your physical and emotionally well-being is the most important concern.

# CHAPTER THREE

## ACQUAINTANCE RAPE AND CAMPUS SEXUAL ASSAULT

Acquaintance rape, also known as date rape, is an extremely serious and widespread problem. It occurs when what appears to be a friendly, innocent sexual overture suddenly becomes a sexual attack.

Research indicates that between fifteen and thirty percent of all women have raped by an acquaintance. Moreover, up to eighty-eight percent of all rapes involve acquaintance, and between fifty-eight and eighty percent of all rapes are perpetrated by an acquaintance while on a date. Far more common than rape by an unknown assailant, this type of "friendly" rape is just as horrible and demeaning.

### INCIDENT

Acquaintance rape can involve relatives, social companions, casual friends, co-workers and other people familiar with each other. The average age of those involved in incidents of date rape, either as perpetrator or victims, is eighteen and a half years. Research also shows that three-quarters of the men and a half of the women involved in acquaintance rape had been drinking alcohol at the time of the assault. But familiarity does not necessarily equal safety, women must therefore always be cautious and alert.

## CHARACTERISTICS OF AN ACQUAINTANCE RAPIST

The best defense against acquaintance rape is the ability to identify and avoid men who are likely to engage in sexual assault. Potential rapists tend to think it is an acceptable means of attaining and resolving disputes. They often have problems with alcohol and /or drugs. They tend to display minimal respect for other human beings generally and they may be cruel to animals and children.

They intrude on the personal space of others, psychological and physically. These men act "macho" they exhibit sexist conduct and attitudes. They will be satisfied with nothing less than complete control of their 'dates' mind and body.

## AVOIDING DATE RAPE

Experts say early warning signals for social rape are intimidating stares, standing too close, enjoying your discomfort, acting as if he knows you better than he does, calling you names that makes you uncomfortable, constantly blocking your way and following you. Touching you in sensitive places "by accident," ignoring what you say and becoming angry when you disagree with him.

## SUGGESTIONS FOR PROTECTING YOURSELF

1. Always maintain a measure of reserve and distance on the first date. This does not mean that you should be cold, uncooperative or impersonal. You can be dignified and at the same time warm, compassionate and understanding.

2. For your first date, arrange to meet him at the location, which should be a public place like a movie theatre, museum, library, mall, coffee shop or restaurant. Insist on a cab or public transportation avoid driving with him, especially in his car.

3. Make certain you take along enough money for a taxi and telephone calls.

4. Consult your friends or any other people who know the person before you accept a date with him.

5. Be certain you know the name of every man you date, where he lives, and something about his occupation. Take his phone number, but do not give your own.

6. Never invite a man in the street, a bar, or any other public place to be alone with you in your residence or any other private place until you know him.

7. Ensure that you are sober on all dates. Alcohol and drugs lower inhibitions and set the stage for unwanted sexual behavior, which can easily turn into sexual assault.

8. Offer to pay for part of the date, or arrange to go "dutch," so that you set a tone of equality.

9.  Should the two of you decide to go someplace isolated or private on your first date, be sure to tell someone before you go and be certain your date knows you have done so.
10. Be wary about strong drugs such as "roofies" or Rhypnol known as the "date-rape" drug, which can be added to your drink without your knowledge.

PRE-EMPTIVE ACTION

Be able to identify danger signals, and be alert to any strange behavior on the part of your date.

Is he trying too hard to convince you to accompany him to an isolated location?

Has he suddenly steered the conversation toward sex?

Is he making lewd statements or describing sexual acts in detail?

Is he using foul language?

Does he suddenly try to hug, kiss, hold or touch you without permission or warning?

Does he start to push and hit you lightly?

Once you are aware of any of these signals, the next steps are crucial in keeping the situation under control.

If you have made a strenuous objection and your date does not stop the behavior, threaten to call the police.

Be assertive and firm in your tone of voice and the body language. Trust your instincts. Lethargy and passivity send the wrong signals, especially to the "macho" type. Ambiguous signals tend to confuse your date, making it more difficult to stop sexual improprieties later.

Do not allow the would-be rapist a small liberty in hope it will prevent further aggression. Remember, acquaintance rape like any rape by a stranger, is mainly an expression of violence in which the assailant seeks to dominate the victim. A token concession is unlikely to stop him.

CONFRONTATION

If these measures have been unsuccessful in dissuading your date from forcing himself on you sexually, there some additional strategies that may work as well with an acquaintance rapist as with a stranger.

USE A VERBAL DEFENSE

Try to talk the rapist out of the attack. Use a conversation as a stalling tactics. Convince him that you do not want sex under any circumstances, with him or anyone else. Explain to him that what he intends is rape. This approach is more effective with an acquaintance or date than with a stranger.

## INVENT A SURPRISE

Another strategy is to tell the attacker that you're having your period or that you feel sick. Tell him that you feel nauseated and are going to throw up. If you can make yourself vomit, do so. Try to make the attacker disgusted. Strange or bizarre behavior may also throw a date-rapist off guard. Rant and rave, flail your hands, make sudden body movement, act out hallucinations.

## ESCAPE

You should think of these strategies as ways to buy time until you figure out an escape. As soon as he lets his guard down, run out of the house or apartment or get out of the car. Attract the attention of other people if possible, scream if you have to. Or tell him you have to go to the bathroom and will be right back then leave through the bathroom window. Telephone for assistance if you can. The best time for you to attempt an escape is at the beginning of the confrontation. During the first few seconds or moments the date rapist will try to get you under his control. The further the situation escalates, the more important the maintaining of that control will become for the rapist and the more difficult it will be to pry yourself loose.

## SELF PROTECTION ON CAMPUS

The two most significant factors associated with campus rape are, how often a women dates and the sobriety (or lack thereof) of her date or acquaintance, as well as herself. The more men she dates, the more likely she will find herself with a man with the characteristics of an assailant. Also, if a woman does drink, she should do so in moderation and stop before she feels dizzy or high. She should find out what her tolerance is before exposing herself to potentially dangerous social situations.

Adherence to the following rules will provide some protection from campus date rape:

Ask a female friend or campus security officer to accompany you home after a late-night party if alcohol has made you dizzy or tired.

Leave immediately with a girlfriend if you find yourself one of the few women at a party.

If your date engages in behavior that makes you feel uncomfortable, be assertive. Tell him if he does not stop, you will end the date.

Memorize the campus security or emergency telephone number.

Refrain from dating "macho" men who demean women.

Avoid parties where alcohol and drugs are consumed, if you drink know your limit.

# HOW TO AVOID GETTING RAPED

Be extremely selective in the men you date. Be aware of any signs that may signal a tendency toward assaultive behavior.

Be on guard when dating athletes or fraternity brothers, particularly first-year students, and especially during first semester in college.

Following are some simple precaution that will provide initial protection for students who enter college.

## A CHECKLIST

1. Have a well-prepared defense plan before you go out, in case your date becomes dangerous. It is important to remain calm and clear-headed when confronted with this situation.
2. Never blame yourself for a sexual assault. Rape is the fault of the attacker, no one else.
3. Remember that the most favorable moment for escape is during the first few seconds of the attack.
4. On a date, be alert to behavior that often precedes a date rape, including attempts to take you to an isolated location, physical contact without your permission, and an over emphasis on sex talk and play. If this happens, try to get away from your date any way you can.
5. Be selective in your dating choice. Avoid men who exhibit the personal characteristics of a potential

rapist. These include men who espouse violence, who demean and control women and who are obsessed with guns, drugs and alcohol.

6. Never remain at a party where you are the only female.

7. Be assertive and say 'no' if your date insists on unwanted sexual comments and touching. Terminate the date immediately if the man becomes physically or sexually aggressive.

8. In the aftermath of a sexual attack, get to a safe place or area, call someone you trust, a friend, a relative or teacher and tell about the assault.

9. Preserve all evidence and refrain from eating, drinking, washing, douching, brushing your teeth and combing your hair.

10. Seek medical help.

11. Seeking counseling by highly trained therapists. Join a support group and share experiences.

12. Be especially alert to 'rape hazards' like isolated places, first dates, and weekend parties.

# HOW TO AVOID GETTING RAPED

# ABOUT THE AUTHOR

Christopher Robinson is the author of five book on personal security. They cover Robbery, Car Jacking, Kidnapping Prevention and this new booklet on How to Avoid Getting Raped.

Christopher has worked as a Teacher of General Science he has training also in, Interview and Interrogation, Retail Loss Prevention from the international Foundation for Protection Officer, Loss Prevention Officer at Guardsman Limited, Atlas and PrimeGuard. He has also worked as Zone supervisor/Sales Representative, Operation Manager and Trainer at Integral Protective Technology. He is presently C.E.O. at Spetsnaz Security Research a Security Consulting and Research Firm, that specialized in background investigation.

# HOW TO AVOID GETTING RAPED

Christopher Robinson